He *Loves* Me Not...

What To Do When Online Dating Hurts

Winsome Duncan

Published by

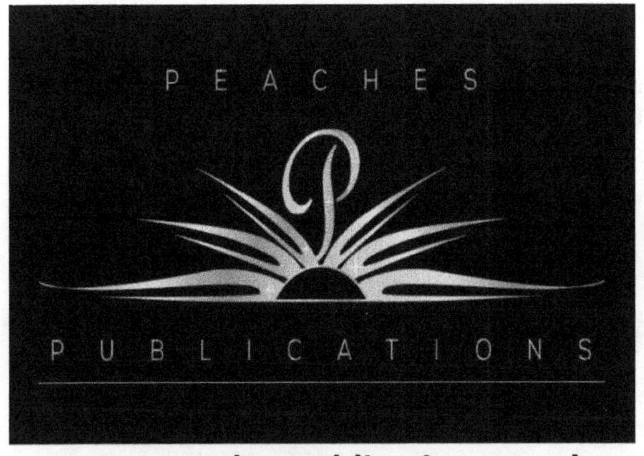

www.peachespublications.co.uk

Published in London by Peaches Publications, 2019.

www.peachespublications.co.uk

British Library Cataloguing in Publication Data: A catalogue record for this book is available from the British Library.

ISBN: 9780955489082

Book cover design: Peaches Publications.

Editor and Typesetter: Winsome Duncan.

Proofreader and Critical Friend: Joanna Oliver.

Table of Contents

WE NEED YOU!!!

Remember to like,

rate and share

HE LOVES ME NOT...

with your loved ones and friends. Leave us an Amazon comment, telling us what you think.

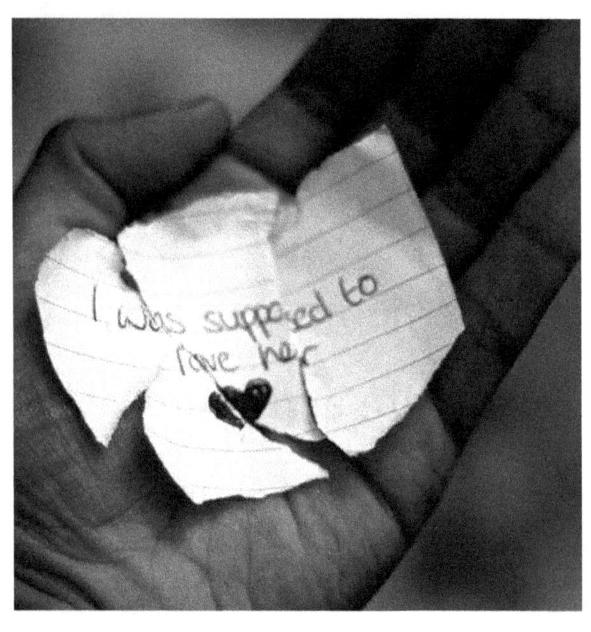

I am just being me
Take me or leave me
You will soon see
My opinions and feelings
need to be free

W. Duncan

Dedication

This book is dedicated to my mum Pat Bayley. Thank you for wiping away my tears, listening on the phone, all your wise advice, hugs, the home cooked meals and input into this book. I am because you are.

A mother's love is unlike any other.

Foreword

By Nicole Reid

Author of 'So You Think I'm Superwoman?'

He Loves Me Not… is a wealth of useful experiences and expertise in the online dating arena. Winsome's willingness to share her vulnerability with others as her journey unfolds, is endearing and has given me hope as I step back out into the dating world. Not only does she portray real honesty in her words, she encourages single ladies to prepare for the advanced social media and technological age and what could happen, as well as how to avoid pitfalls.

As a Transition Coach, I talk about overcoming the breakup of a marriage and how to move on from a broken heart, when the other half said "forever" in their wedding vows. I teach women how to love themselves again, helping them to find their self-worth and value. I am a specialist in creating vision boards and writing books, as it is important to know what type of guy we are looking for. Using visual aids such as vision boards, to highlight the qualities of your perfect guy, can prove to be very useful. They can be a point of reference when beginning to see those red flags, as Winsome shares in the chapter 'Empty Hole'.

As an author of two awarding winning books: 'So, You Think I'm Superwoman?' and poetry book, 'Words Never Said', I understood the need to show women globally, how to work on new goals as well as getting ourselves back 'out there'. I teach techniques on how to start socialising with confidence, especially with men and help women to regain trust and find love again. Starting a new chapter of your life does not need to be daunting.

He Loves Me Not... explores an increasingly popular way of meeting new people, online. We have the opportunity to talk to potential partners, build a rapport, begin dating and with a bit of luck, find the man of our dreams, via social media dating apps. This is a new craze and apparently, everyone is doing it, unless you live under a rock! Whether you are new to the game, like me or have not been successful so far, there are so many things to consider, including common sense matters, which seem to fly out of our pretty little heads when hearing some hot, buttery, sweet talk. Maybe being given attention for the first time in a long while, is so flattering that we flip into temporary insanity mode. What happens next when we go on a great date and then the guy just ups and disappears off the face of the planet? How do we emotionally cope with that form of rejection? What happens next, when he swears you are the one, and that he wants to marry you after one month? Where do you go from there, when your deepest need is to be in a loving healthy relationship and to start a family? This can be emotionally challenging to handle, so ladies: pay attention.

Initially I was quite sceptical about talking to people, searching for companionship and 'finding love' online. I had put the idea off for some time, declaring that online dating was not for an old-timer like me. Lack of knowledge and horror stories about catfishing and mother saying, "you could meet a murderer", kept me far away from it all and scared me stupid. To be fair, you could go to a night club, meet someone and they turn out to be a nasty piece of work, so what is the difference? Finally, I gave into my niece's request of, "Auntie, let me make you a profile" and I stepped out boldly and thought to try something new and exciting, even if it is bloody scary. The need to be desired and wanted by somebody magnified and 'somebody' called louder than the lonely nights at home. Quite frankly, my late night phone calls of, "no, you hang up.." has been dry for quite some time.

This book has its light and shade, as there are many success stories out there, with people meeting online and going on to live drama-free. However, it does contain mostly precautionary measures to consider before diving in with your heart first and eyes wide shut, whatever stage of dating you are at. He Loves Me Not... can only serve as a tool to navigate yourself when dating online.

We are all healing from past hurts, relationships and experiences and you need not be locked up in your house, waiting for Mr Right or any Mr to wander along and sweep you off your feet. You have to put yourself out there again and again and kiss a whole heap of frogs, until you meet your heart match. You will either have a funny story to tell when the tears dry, or it will be fun while it lasts. You won't get any feedback, staying stagnant. I appreciate the way Winsome has placed her experiences into this narrative, in order for it to be read, referred back to and kept as a handy guide throughout all the stages of this online dating world. I wish I had read this copy before my online dating journey started because it would have served me well. My experience has not put me off dating men online and it's never too late to make more informed decisions before putting all your eggs, hopes and dreams in one basket. This book is best suited as a travel companion, a bath time read or a girly night in, with a glass of wine and some giggles. Always trust your gut instincts and remember The Only Way To Do It, Is To Do It, with the He Loves Me Not... book always in the back of your memory bank archive.

Nicole Reid

Being Single

Is

Not A Curse

Introduction

WARNING THIS IS NOT YOUR AVERAGE

ONLINE DATING BOOK!

Great, now we have the formalities out of the way, trick or treat? Hell, it might just be a Rocky Horror show! Dating life is often compared to a box of chocolates, some sweet indulgences can get stuck in your teeth and can cause tooth decay, while other sweets are plain Janes and leave a bitter crunch and unpleasant coffee breath aftertaste. We are not decrepit yet and still can shake that thang on the disco dancefloor before we become relics.

Holy cow! Moomoo has gone woowoo, now you're a MAD, ANGRY DATING COW, date life can get like that sometimes; can I be real with you? We get on with a man, no problem meeting a man, then we fall apart because he is just not that into us. We trip over his woven lies like, "I'm not married" or, "I'll call you right back" and like our friend Humpty Dumpty, we all fall down and proceed to get back up and fly like super woman. But wait there is more, we leave Humpty Dumpty in pieces on the floor because we can't put him back together again, when really those pieces are us feeling shattered, battered and humiliated. Can I get a witness? Don't worry, be happy, you will get over it. Sit back, click your seat belt because reading this book is going to be a bumpy side-splitting ride.

Ladies, let us face FACTS; the world of online dating will be one of the scariest things you will ever have to do in your lives. Think about it logically, you are meeting a practical stranger with no frame of reference, who might not even be who he appears to be or look like the image in the photograph… also known as a Catfish. Online dating is synthetic and one of the most unnatural processes of meeting new people. Then there are the online dating safety aspects, that you seriously need to consider. In today's modern traumatic world, mental health is on the increase, domestic violence is on the rise and you are exposing yourself to potentially devious characters, of which you do not even know. There were no family or friend's present making the dating introduction, who can vouch that he is not a psycho. So, you must have your wits about you. My name is Winsome Duncan and I have been called a **serial dater**; what a bloody cheek. However, truth be told, I do know a little something, something about the bizarre world of online dating. As a busy powerhouse entrepreneur, I have chosen to date online for the past ten years and I've been on approximately 50 dates. In my field, I find most men to be intimidated by my intense personality or they are just plain unavailable. Despite my efforts not to be an man-woman.

If you are luckily enough to find the perfect match, he can make you see planets, the moon and stars. His love can take you around the world but first you must let him capture you. That is why it is called THE CHASE; ladies - men love to hunt. It is in their DNA. **You man, I woman.** If you are reading this book, you have one of two problems, either you are:

A. **New to online dating**
B. **Unsuccessful at online dating**

Either way, this book is definitely for you. I share my personal experiences, insights and I think I know enough to get you started on the path to courting safely, should you decide that you want to give cyber-dating a whirl.

Serial Dater

Yeah about that. There were two key factors that happened to me, which inspired me to write this book. The first was a message from....well let's call him 'Mr Echo'. I opened my dating app and it read:

Mr Echo: Do you remember me?

Winsome: No. Remind me.

Mr Echo: We went out on a date together.

Winsome: Oh really. Where did we go?

Mr Echo: To a Japanese restaurant but it was closed. So, we went to eat in Le Bodgetia.

Winsome: Okay.

Mr Echo: Why did you date me without any intention of seeing me. You are just a serial dater.

#UNMATCH (ouch)

Winsome: What the fuck?

Mr Echo had touched a nerve and really hurt my feelings; I actually burst into tears. In fact, I was balling the house down. I felt awful that I left that impression on him, when I know that all I ever wanted was to be loved. If that is what he thought, what did my other dates think? The thing about it was Mr Echo was not that memorable and he was short, small and mouseish looking. He probably wanted me to come to his house on the second date and I was just not interested. I wanted so badly to retort, so I had to become a Lady Detective and find out what his Facebook account was.

Yep you guessed it, I googled him. Found him and sent him the following message:

Winsome: I felt really upset when you called me a serial dater. It actually hurt my feelings. You should not judge others, especially as you are still on the dating app yourself; people call names to who they really are. I had a break from dating and was in a relationship for a while. My whole life does not evolve around this app. If we went on a date and we did not click, maybe that was not God's plan for us. Maybe I should have been more upfront and told you that I was not interested. Anyway, I've said my piece. I hope you find what you are looking for.

Good luck.

Mr Echo: Sorry about that. But it was how I felt at the time and to think you didn't even recognise me made me conclude. However, I shouldn't have. Sorry about that and good luck.

Winsome: I apologise too. I do hope you meet your queen.

Mr Echo: Thanks and I hope you meet your Prince charming too.

I shit you not, this was a real-life transcript of our Facebook conversations. After this interaction, it got me thinking about my dating life, how I have used online dating to meet most of my partners and in particular, what I wish I knew prior to online dating. I am a busy entrepreneur and do not have time to meet men in society's so-called 'traditional' ways. Online dating is instant access, quick and fun. You meet many different personalities and one thing is for certain, you get to become really clear about what you are looking for in a potential partner. Looking back, if you are going to use online dating apps, I would suggest that you use ones you need to pay for, as the quality of men is better. A professional who pays for a dating site is less likely to want sexual hook ups and does not have a free-for-all mentality.

The second key factor motivating this book was a chance encounter with a dickhead who worked in a Caribbean take away shop, in New Cross London, England. He had mocha skin, which glistened over the hot coals, where he was cooking BBQ jerk chicken. He had muscles for days and was physically fit - the 'type' of man I'm attracted to. At this point, I need to call myself foolish, a foolish fool. He asked me to meet up at midnight, after his shift finished and we sat and talked in my car till 4am. He was too cheap to buy a £4 drink but he did bring some food and drink, which he probably stole from the shop. Yes, the alarms bells did go off but in my head, I was thinking, 'he is so fine and he is my type of guy and it's a hot summer's evening. Who knows? He could be the one!' We giggled like school children and he was really interesting to talk to. Then the conversation suddenly turned to steamy heights and he began to tell me how I'm his sized-type of woman and that he wants to go downtown and eat me out. By this time, I was feeling quite moist down there, flushed in my cheeks and the back window was steaming up. It was at this point I better go and find my yard (home).

Short end to this story

He figured out I was not going to give up the cookie, though he nobly tried. I did not hear from him for one week and I'm thinking, 'what the backfoot?'. I called a couple of times and I kept getting his voicemail, until one day I decided to call him on a private number (men hate that); I don't business, pick up your phone, you knob head! To my dismay, it rang and went to voicemail. He blocked me from calling him, I could not believe it. Then the cray cray lady came out (crazy lady); I called his job and I'm like, "how dare you?" Why could he not just make up a lie and say, "it's not you, it's me" and everyone can get on with their merry lives. He was shocked I called him and started stuttering on the phone. I asked him directly, "Why did you block me?" and he just began mumbling, "I'm at work, I don't want to see you etc, blah blah, blah." It gets boring at times, you know. Imagine if I'd slept with him on a whim, he would have been Houdini's best disappearing act.

Again, I felt hurt like a wounded dog sitting in the corner, especially because I loved that take-away food and I attend there often! I stopped and wondered, 'Why, oh why do I keep creating these situations, with men looking for a cheap date or some cheap ass?' I know, I know I can hear you judging, 'well you should not be meeting midnight men'. Unfortunately, at that point in my life, I was a heavy weed user and my thoughts were erratic, hazy, and lonely, so really, I was not in my right mind. I believe meeting Mr Dickhead was one of those defining moments in my life and as I sat down and told my mum of my dating woes, she said, "You should write a book!" That night, I got out my laptop and we both sat down created the concepts you are about to read here. We laughed and I cried a lot along the way, as I documented tear by tear, what to be painfully aware of, when dating online. I hope you enjoy this quick read and may it serve as guide to keeping safe. Go grab a banana, let's dance and drink some moonshine!

Being Single
Is
Self-Discovery

What Happened To The Good Ole Days?

Call me old fashioned if you want to; I do not care what you call me but tell me this? What ever happened to:

- A blind date introduction
- Meeting a potential date in person
- Courting a lady

- A gentleman walking you home after a date
- A gentleman calling your house before seven o'clock
- Holding your hand being a huge sexual advance
- A kiss on the cheek being like foreplay
- A man asking your father for your hand in marriage
- What happened to the second, third, fourth, and fifth dates?
- Your date being scared to meet your parents (oh wait, that one still exists.)

Online dating is like a packet soup, it is instant gratification in a phone, just mix with hormones and away we go. We can log in and connect with someone based on our lust and sexual appetite, without really knowing some of the two-foot devils we speak with. We do not know who they are or what is their agenda and even if they are genuine. Nowadays we are bombarded by virtual sex, pornography, sexualised advertisements, sex toys, sex shops, dildos, 24-hour WhatsApp messages contact, online dating sites and so much more. It is unnatural I say; we are no longer left with the romance and intrigue of meeting someone new, the pounding hearts and the sweaty palms.

Modern dating has now become sordid, seedy and shady. Online dating has become a cesspool of iniquity and sexually transmitted diseases, oh sorry, sexually transmitted *infections* is now the correct terminology, beg your pardon. With all this going on, are we really any happier in our dating lives? I think not. Technically you are taking a risk when you date online and I am going to give it to you straight, no chaser.

What, who and where is safe in this day and age of corrupt thinking, group sex and fornication? Don't get me wrong, I'm not a prude, however I am sick and fed up to the bloody back teeth of women wanting to find true love, falling into the traps of online dating predators, who lay in waiting to take your most precious nectar. If I can help you avoid feeling like a mug, wherever possible, then I will do my best to uphold my promise to share information. Welcome to the world of online dating, a mythical place for hunters to catch their prey and if I do not tell you, then who will?

I personally have been on approximately 50 online dates over the past decade, an average of 5 dates per year. Until Mr Echo caused me to examine my dating history and really question whether, other than a free dinner, what was my real payoff here? Yes, I was wounded that he called me a serial dater and as I mentioned before, I did not remember him; I certainly did not remember that he took me on a date. He was actually quite forgettable! What I do remember he looked nothing like his pictures, at a best guess, some photoshop trickery must have occurred because his skin pigment had changed. Colourism is alive and well and it affects women and men globally. Some white people are trying to tan and appear darker and some black people are trying to appear shades lighter. It would seem to me that many are not comfortable in their skin. When it comes down to it, if the date you meet looks significantly different in person, how do you address that without causing offense?

The comment, "I think you are a serial dater" made me cry for one week and I thought to myself, 'that is not who I am'. I *have* had relationships from online dating. I was offended, shocked and horrified that I left that impression on someone, all because I did not want to go on a second date. Listen hear, I want to be loved from the crown of my head to the soles of my feet, like any other well-balanced female out there. I want to be in a long-term relationship with my booboo. However, I'll be real with you, in my experience the quality of men in online dating can be substandard. My best guess is that men being or feeling lonely, drives them to open an account and their emptiness just becomes magnified online. So, the search does not become to genuinely meet a partner, the search becomes to fill the empty hole and it is more about being a conquerer and how many ladies he can bag because he is probably a fuckboi. Now if you want to wake up with an itch in the morning, by all means do go ahead and listen to the shit they tell you but do not say I haven't warned you. Am I bitter? No. Do I have issues in my tissues? For sure I do. I'm still working out my stuff, after stopping my heavy marijuana use for 3 years my view is starting to clear.

Don't get me wrong, I know of two relationships that worked out through meeting online, so it can happen on rare occasions. One relationship is in its fourth year and the other resulted in a marriage. It is possible to find happiness, all is not lost and a positive outlook is the correct way to go about the business of attracting a good man to you. I just want to give you an opportunity to get it right, based upon the insights of some of my previous foolish mistakes. It is official, the good ole days have gone, so let's start in this technological age. If you're not too scared out of your wits at this point, let's continue on....

There Is Purpose In Your Pain

Is Online Dating For You?

Why do people opt for dating online? Normally it is because we believe we do not have the time or energy to date via introduction. We are super-important and super-busy. Just like online shopping, we log online, view who we want and select that particular experience. Online dating has become a convenient way to meet a potential suitor, it does not take much effort to go out on a date. Men and women who use online dating may use it for many different reasons, here are some examples:

1. To fall in love and get married
2. To find a long-term relationship
3. Sex hook-ups
4. Swingers who are looking for an additional sex partner (I kid you not)
5. To gain citizenship and receive a passport or green card
6. Friendship
7. To avoid feelings of being lonely
8. To counteract personal difficulties in meeting new people
9. To regain confidence in dating, after a traumatic breakup
10. To save time

Having been an online dater for more than ten years now, I do believe that you need to be thick-skinned for this process. The one **Golden Rule** I wish for you to remember during this process is:

Who you see online, may not be what they appear in real life.

Do yourself a favour and heed those words. This will be crucial in all your future internet interactions. Please log that in your long-term memory vault. Thank you, please.

Just because a man's profile says he is self-employed does not mean he is self-employed. Remember the online world can be deceiving and becomes a fantasy world to the best imaginations on earth. I have had first-hand experiences with men who said they have no children only to see dodgy Roger in Barclays bank with his son and daughter around his ankles saying, "daddy, daddy". When he was confronted by me, it was like he lost his words in the air and looking down at the floor became his best friend. Another example was broke-teeth Chippy, who said he had one son and when we broke up suddenly 2 more girl children appeared. His response was that he was protecting his girl children from me. And I am thinking, 'what about the Gucci and Prada sunglasses locked away in your safe, do you need to protect them as well?' Looking back, I now realised why, when he got paid every two weeks, he had no money left....because of his family responsibilities! He was talking jive about he's building a house back home in Nigeria and how he has to send money to his parents. I believed him because I wanted to believe in something, until his grunts got louder when he was angry and was prepared to spend more time in the gym than to come and see me. And let's not forget everything wrong in our relationship was my fault. Ladies, when you have low self-esteem it eats away at the core of your confidence, trust me. Put not your trust in man and know your worth as a woman.

Another time, a guy who I will call 'Huggie Bear' swore blind he was single, only for me to find out weeks later, he was separated from his WIFE; what the fuck? Ladies think about it, if he is married, he is NOT single. Geez! Lord help me!

Let me explain something to you, when a man says any of the following:

- I am married but it's not working out
- I live with my baby mama but we are not sleeping together
- I am married but we are separated

- I am in the process of getting a divorce
- I can't invite you round because I live at my mum's house
- It's complicated (a classic)

Girlllllllllll pleeeeeeeease, put on your Usain Bolt trainers and run lightning speed in the opposite direction. Come on ladies, your parents did not write 'muggins' on your birth certificate. Any of the above means this man IS NOT AVAILABLE. Period. Full stop. The end! He belongs to someone else, until that decree nisi comes through in the post. Chances are he will go back to her or that he just has a lot of emotional baggage and just wants to fool around and get his dick wet. It was really hard to walk away from Huggie Bear because he was my kind of fine, tall, handsome and strong. However, the alarm bells just kept on ringing, until the red flag was waving in the wind. Here they were:

First Alarm Bell: He did a no-show for one of our dates and gave some whack excuse about his friend being arrested by police.

Second Alarm Bell: He just would not talk or open up. My mamma said, “still waters run deep”. Huggie Bear was not a good conversationalist, which bothered me and that was just a deal breaker.

Third Alarm Bell: We had been on quite a few dates and one night the way he kissed me, then went on to devour my chin, as if we were in the bedroom having sex, made me feel very uncomfortable. He don’t know me like that!

Fourth Alarm Bell: His wife called the police on him and accused him of abusing her. My first thought was that where there is smoke, there is fire. Up to this day, he stills messages me on snapchat on occasion. I wonder if he is divorced yet?

My gut was telling me that he had the potential to be violent. Although I had never experienced such things with him, I had to listen to my inner guide. It was telling me not to go any further with this man. It was hard, he really liked me and he was separated from his wife for one year at the time. Not an official separation, just living apart. You see the thing nowadays, is that common sense is not that common anymore. You need to be fully informed about what you are getting into. Especially as you do not want any crazy wives on your doorstep.

Push Past The Pain

Because Your Next Stop

Is Greatness

The Empty Hole

It hurts here, say hello. I'm feeling 2 shades of purple pain when he does not call. A numb void echoes in the wind and I am displaced in my quest of love once again. Remembering past heartbreak, my soul aches for a better tomorrow. A real union, not strengthened by lust, angry sex and humiliation. I have a theory; it is quite simple. The majority of online daters have missing pieces within and their soul is not whole. In fact, they are broken in some way, shape or form. Yes, this includes myself. Let's be honest, online dating is one of the most synthetic ways to meet a prospect or lover. It is a radioactive screen, with empty messages leading to a quick tumble and then on to the next or on occasion, a Happy Ever After. We do have some fairy tales, by no means do I want to be the voice of doom and gloom in this book; what I do want is to be a realist. What online dating does is disconnect you from meeting the core soul, mind and energy vibrations that you would naturally occurs when meeting in person, face to face.

It hurts because I turned to online dating to fill that ache, when really what I needed to do was to love **me more**. Surfing my way through a mass of online profiles never satisfied my soul, it just gave me something to do. It numbed the pain of loneliness. 'Oh, look at me my phones bleeping, he loves me, he loves me not'. Now we are unmatched. Our pre-dating conversations failed the standard. Unrequited love is a bitch that slaps you upside the head, when you believe you found the one. If you are feeling broken inside and you cry tears on your interior, maybe online dating is not right for you at this point. Simply put, you will only attract more of who you are and what you are feeling. Trust me, it's a word from the wise. Alcoholics, drug users and wife beaters will all turn up to take you out on your first date. Lauren Hill said, 'How you gonna win, when you ain't right within?' Girl I'll drink to that. Cheers.

In this chapter my point is this, if you are looking for online dating to fix the broken you, relieve the lonely nights or to make you feel wanted, it's probably not for you. As mama said, "I can see up the street and around the corner". The darker side of this type of dating can leave your self-confidence on the floor shattered into a million pieces; it can give you sleepless nights of 'why did I not get to a second date?' If you're not mentally tough enough to handle rejection, online dating will eat you alive.

The Come Down

Like a flat can of coke, you lose all your gas when you realise the man of your dreams is not what he seems. You hear the familiar sound of your heart shattering into a trillion segments. Your soul glow light dims faintly in the distance and you cry a river into your ice cream tub. My sister, please be still, focus and get with it when **he tells you:**

- It's not you, it's me
- I'm too busy for a relationship right now but we can chill
- I don't see this going anywhere
- You seem like you want a serious relationship
- I got too much in my head right now
- Or he just goes ghost on you

To Thine Own Self, Be True

Self-love is key to the quest of happiness and only begins if you feel ready to socialise, meet and greet your dates. If you are not careful, online dating can become a distraction to your current situation or worse still, there is a danger you will become obsessed. I wrote this book because I am tired of the Ray Ray & Poki experience. I need a real man in my life. A man that is:

- ✓ Strong
- ✓ Caring
- ✓ Kind
- ✓ Considerate
- ✓ An attentive listener
- ✓ Loyal
- ✓ Faithful
- ✓ Humorous
- ✓ Loving
- ✓ Focused
- ✓ Affectionate
- ✓ Respectful
- ✓ Patience

These are some of the traits that I have put on my vison board. Along with images of me being happy, in love, secure and in a family. You too can create a relationship vision board, from magazine articles and press cuttings. Call into existence those things that are not yet seen. Have an optimistic approach. Be honest about your deal breakers and what you will and will not accept. If you still want to online date, now you are ready to finally take the next step and create a profile.

When It Hurts, Cry

Creating A Profile

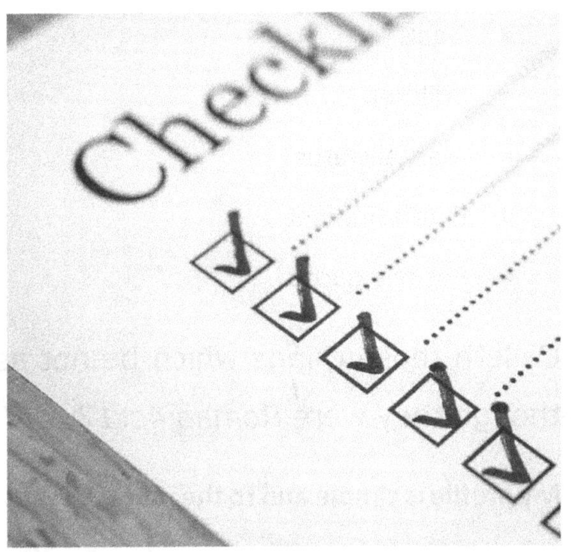

Your profile needs to be positive, upbeat and uplifting. Do not talk about what you do not want, talk about what you do want and what you do like. Here is a list of topics you could cover:

- Hobbies
- Occupation

- Likes
- Animals
- Goals
- Children
- Marital status
- Entertainment
- Positive quote

Calleth those things which be not as though they were *Roman 4c:17vKJV*.

My profile is simple and to the point, it reads:

I'm looking forward to stimulating conversation and having a good laugh. I believe laughter is healing medicine. Swipe right if this resonates with you. I enjoy live music, movies, comedy nights and eating out. I am a good listener, driven, focused and enjoy a good conversation.

I'm a lover of the English language. U is spelt you, ur is spelt your and r is spelt are. I will only response to standard English messages. (my deal breaker)

Only well-balanced emotionally-connected men need apply.

Thank you.

Be mindful of men who do not write anything or very little on their profiles. If they can't be bothered to write a little about themselves, is that the type of character you want to date?

The 3-Step Dating System

How To Date Online Safely

A picture tells a thousand words, if you look close enough. In the first instance, you must use your eyes, instincts and inner guide to help find yourself a potential suitor. You can tell so much by the images he puts online. The key thing to remember here is if a man dates you 3 times or more, he is emotionally invested in you. Let that be the bullseye target you are aiming for.

This section is broken down into 3 core areas:

1. Round One – Ding Ding!

From the gate, it is advisable that you implement as many, if not all, the points that I raise in this section, especially if you are a newbie to the dating world. This will help give you a grounding and a solid foundation in your pursuit to online dating.

2. Second Base – Touch-Me-Nots

In this section, you are both interested in each other and discovering the options of pursuing a relationship. You are probably intimate with one another and deciding when is the right time to go skin-to-skin.

3. Home Run – Forever My Lady

Congratulations if you have arrived here. Well done. Good luck. You're not home free just yet and you need to do a few final checks, just to make sure you're really secured.

'Think About It' Alert

Whenever I say THINK ABOUT IT, I would really like you to take a moment to sit down and ponder what I have just written. Ladies, let's get our brains in gear and get our hearts and minds right and prepare for our King. These are my dating life lessons learnt, so with that said, let's get to it.

Round

One

Rule #1: Do not go to his house on the first date

Sounds simple enough but I feel I need to point out the obvious. Remember, you do not know this man from a can of paint. Why would you put yourself in danger to go to his home on a first date, that's not really a date because it is in his home? Scrap that idea of a first date meet up because even if he is cooking you dinner at his home, it is not an official date until you both go out in a public place and he puts his hand in his wallet and buys you a one drink minimum. Love yourself enough to know that your safety is paramount.

Rule #2: Remember rule number 1 - do not go to his house on the first date UNDER ANY CIRCUMSTANCES

Just in case you forgot rule number 1 let me remind you, meet in a public place during the day or early evening, on a first date. You hear of these awful stories of women being murdered or raped by a random stranger that they met online. Even if your confidence and self-esteem is on the floor and you are grateful for the interest, this is never an ideal option. I have made this mistake, so you do not have to.

When I met Rick The Dick, I was so besotted by his good looks that all of my sense flew out of the window. We finally arranged our first date and I asked to meet an hour later because I was preoccupied at another engagement and he point-blank refused to reschedule. A whole year would go by with us having intermittent communications and mini arguments along the way.

We had been speaking and video calling on and off for a year, so you can imagine my false sense of security. I let him pursue me and chase, however the deal breaker was he requested to only meet me at his home, which I declined for 12 months. He was quite intense and controlling, which of course I interpreted as manly. Isn't it strange how some women can create a new frame of reference to accommodate what we really want to hear a man say, or to excuse poor behaviour?

When I foolishly decided to comply and went to his home, being strangled and having a gun pointed at me was never part of the plan. I will reveal more of how I got myself entangled into this scenario later.

Rule #3: Catchy Profiles

A man that takes the time to put some thought into his profile and write more than one word, is worth considering. If he bothers to read your profile and makes reference to what you have written, he is worth talking to. A key trick here is to make sure you mention a secret code for them to mention in a message, for example your profile could read at the end: *Be sure to mention 'BlackKnight', so I know you have read all the way to the end of my profile. This will guarantee a response.*

This is a great opener and for him to impress you by paying attention to details.

Rule #4: Full Body Shots

Make sure you have a least one full length body shot on your profile pictures. Aim to have a variety of close ups and different poses. Upload a minimum of 3 pictures and a maximum of 5. Any more than 5, it is hard to keep a man guessing.

Rule #5: Conversation Generator

It can be quite tricky generating conversation in the beginning but not impossible. In general, you need to think about subjects to discuss like:

- Work life
- Family
- Future goals and aspirations
- What is his ideal woman?
- Does he want children?
- Does he want more children?
- What is his moral code?

Be like a Police Officer, it is always helpful to ask the same question twice but in another way. This way you can check if he is being consistent in his answers. For example, when speaking with Mr Houdini, one day he disclosed a time when he got drunk and said but I do not drink often, I logged what he said and was checking for any alcohol addiction. In another conversation a few days later, I asked, "when did you last have a drink" and his response was, "as I told you I don't drink a lot, are you trying to catch me out or something?" and I just laughed. It is a useful technique and takes some time to master, so as not to make a man feel that he is being interrogated.

Rule #6: Can't Spell, Won't Spell

A pet hate of mine is when men use text abbreviations to communicate with me. Call me old skool but it makes my skin crawl. I am a lover of the English language, obviously because I am a writer. I am not a 10-year child in the playground writing love notes saying, 'I luv U'. It should read 'I love you'. This form of broken English tells you a lot about the guy's ability to express himself.

Rule #7: Make Notes

Some online dating apps give you an option to make notes about your thoughts of the person you have matched and have been conversing with. When it comes to speaking on the phone, this is a great way to impress him with key points of how much knowledge you remember about what he has told you and saves confusion with other matches you have spoken to. It also seems like you are paying close attention. Many times, I have been accused of not listening or getting my information muddled.

Rule #8: Tonality

Articulation and dictation are quite key for me because I am a singer, poet and a music lover, this means I hear on a whole different frequency. I hear the high-pitched noise that my car fan makes and the soft grating noise from the suspension going over speed humps. If a man you are getting to know struggles to be coherent, you have to ask yourself the question, “why?”. A man should be able to hold a decent conversation for a good 15 to 20 minutes. If not, find out as quickly as you can, why is he easily distracted. Is he under the influence of drugs and alcohol? Alcoholics slur their words often during sentences and drug users tend to take long pauses, often because they are high or buzzing, so there is a significant delay in your words transmitting to their brain. Look out for distractions, for example; Mr Houdini hung up the phone so quickly when interrupted by his flatmate. Before he left, his famous last words were, "my flatmate is calling me, I will call you back". At this point I began to think is it his flatmate, girlfriend or wife vying for his attention? He never did call me back that evening, so it really makes me ponder, 'was it his flatmate, he spoke to?'

Isn't it funny how some men are unable to pick up a call during certain activities, like the dinner table with family or between 6 p.m. and 11 p.m., which is peak spouse and children time? Or indeed, like in this instance, when speaking to their so-called and possibly imaginary flatmate! Why is it so strange to pick up a call and say, "I'm about to eat, I'll call you back", or "Now is not a good time to talk babe", if you have nothing to hide and then actually surprise me and follow through on calling me back. To me, it is as though their thoughts of you suddenly disappear, like magic, when they have to respond at poignant times of the day or night, as the case may be. Be sure to listen out for that faint female voice in the background, or hearing the famous, “she is just a friend” or “she is my sister” type routine. I dated Mr Pants on Fire for 3 months and I met his sister, only to find out that his sister locks him out of the house all night. He does not want to call his sister because she does not pick up the phone and wants him to shame himself and bang the door down at 4 a.m. in the morning. Think about it? Why would your sister lock you out? Well you have guessed, it was not his sister. A massive glaring red flag for me was at night, he did not want to talk while he was in the house and would come out of his bed to talk to me in the street, with his whispering voice.

When I probed further, he said he did not want to disturb his sister and her daughter but surely that daughter should be called his niece? I'm just saying, watch your back for these low talking, raspberry men who pretend like they are single and ready to mingle. Remember, the aim here is to have all the attention on you when you speak and to find some common ground, whilst establishing a genuine friendship. You can focus on communicating effectively and everybody wins.

Rule #9: Pay Attention

If we cannot measure the entire universe, what makes you believe a guy is telling the truth? If we do not know how many planets are in the entire galaxy, why would you accept what he says as the gospel truth? Remember, you do not know this man. You must pay attention at all times, to the conversation you and your suitor are having. This can give you a clear indication of what their true intentions are. Do not allow your head to become filled with what he thinks you want to hear.

Rule #10: Match Text

If a guy writes a short text:

How are you?

Be sure to match text him word for word. For example, your response could be:

Fine, and you?

Basically, match whatever effort he puts in and do not always respond straight away. Unless it is on WhatsApp and he can blatantly see you online and has a 'double blue ticks' notification that his message has been read. Be comfortable with ending text talk early. Just say you have to get ready to go out or you're cooking dinner. Do not drag out long texts, encourage him to desire you more in your absence as it will make him chase more for your time, if he is genuinely interested.

Rule #11: The Golden Million-Dollar Question

In my experience, you will do well to ask this question early on in the 'getting to know him' stage. Here it is:

Are you single?

It sounds simple enough doesn't it? You will probably get a mixed bag of responses from this man. The most common response is, "why would I be on a dating site if I was not single"? Why indeed....? It is almost laughable. This allows men who are in a partial relationship to consider coming clean to you. You will be surprised how you will find a small number of guys who begin to backtrack and tell you their whole relationship drama of why they are single and how it's complicated but he is really in a relationship or married. For example, Mr Topics was on the site with some nice pictures and over a lovely meal when asked if he was single he responded, "it's complicated". I must have looked stunned, then he said he does not want to talk about it; surprise, surprise. This is where I used my psychic abilities and said, “you either have a girlfriend or a wife” and he responded, “something like that” and changed the subject. After the date ended, he invited me back to his place and said he lives alone. So basically, he was offering me dick and alcohol for a £40 date. Eventually, he confessed and came clean and said he was still married; we scantily keep in touch, enough for him to tell me that he has found two women and has threesomes on a regular basis.

Some men come right out very early on and say they are in a situation, however that it has nothing to do with you. Thank them for being honest and wish them well on their journey and step back from all communication. Why would you not want a loose-dick man, who is not 100% committed to you? THINK ABOUT IT! Once you have asked this question and you discover later on down the line that this man is attached to someone, you can call him out as a straight-up liar. Eventually you will find out when he loses interest and the façade drops. Just because they call you all different times during the day and night means nothing. We go on facts Lady Detectives, yes that's a matter of fact, remember that.

When I met Mr Overground, he was polite, cute and charming. We met at his place of work, at the Overground station, when I was traveling to work. He was hungry in his pursuit of me until eventually I gave him my digits, after our paths crossed a few times. He was eager to take me out on a date but I wanted to talk to him more, it was just a vibe I got. Very early on, my gut told me something was not quite right but I could not figure it out. He was always available to speak and would call back if he was not near his phone. Eventually I agreed to our first dinner date, which he cancelled one hour before we were supposed to meet. He gave me some excuse of someone being on the tracks. Okay Lady Detectives, it is time to hit the pause button here, consider this:

- Your gut is telling you something is not right
- He broke his first arrangement to meet up with you
- When he calls, he is whispering or has a low voice

What could this all possibly mean? Those three signs indicated to me, a red flag. I immediately began to back away and distance myself, he requested another date but I was not really feeling it. A couple weeks later, I saw him in the chicken and chips shop. I went inside to say hello and saw him picking up a call and guess who was on the caller display, yup you guess it, right in front of my eyes, "Wifey" popped up. I could not make this ish up. I was horrified and disappointed. His poor wife, sitting at home thinking, 'I got me a good husband'. I acted like I never saw his phone and greeted him in a loud voice, "Hi, how are you?". Mr Overground told his wifey he would call her back. I said, "who was that"? He responded, "A friend". Then I confronted him about what I saw and how out of order he was, he denied it, so I went to grab for his phone and said, "okay, well let's call wifey back and see what she has to say about it." Yes, you guessed it, he stared down at the floor like it was his best friend, probably praying and wishing it would open up and swallow him. Although we never met online, this clearly shows the importance of asking the golden million-dollar question. Say it with me ladies: "Are you single?" I even go a step further in my initial message and I either get a response or no response, to the following:

Thanks for the match, so tell me are you:

- Single
- Separated
- Divorced

Rule #12: Secondary Number

The man in the moon and his dog can have my secondary number. Take the time to purchase a £1 chip and a cheapo £20 mobile. Use this as your dating hotline. Men do it, so why can't we? It is so important to maintain a healthy distance in the beginning of getting to know a guy. They need to know you are not accessible to them 24-7 and you can have the power to turn off your phone in the evening. This helps to avoid late night texting.

Rule #13: Cut-Off Times

Create a cut-off time to stop texting, message or speaking on the phone. You want to create a demand for your time. Let him pursue and chase you and work up a sweat. This just makes your communication more appealing, when he cannot speak to you every day or you don't respond to his text straight away.

Rule #14: What Does A Man Want?

Ladies, a man wants the following:

- He wants to feel he's in control
- He wants to chase
- He wants to pursue you
- He wants to be the hunter
- He wants a woman who knows when to be quiet
- He wants to be a provider
- He wants to be assured that he is doing okay
- He wants to be able to confide in you

- He wants to have a home-cooked meal

Let him achieve his goal and sit in the driving seat for a while, remember he can think he is the head but we women are the neck, to turn the head. This is not a definitive list but it should give you a clear indicator of what he wants.

Rule #15: Become A Lady Detective

Do you remember the book, 'The Lady Detective' and then the lovely Jill Scott came along and starred in the series, playing the Lady Detective in South Africa? You want to accrue as much information as possible when it comes to considering a suitor for a potential mate. I have always found my private online stakeout helpful in building a picture of who the man really is. Remember, people will always present their best selves and will never reveal straight away, their authentic characters. Remember, knowledge is power and if you can see inconsistencies without him knowing, then it is more grease to your elbows. You do not need to disclose to him that you have built your own profile. Here are my 'stakeout tips', to get you started on the road to truth:

1. Type his name into google and check his profile status online.

Ideally, you will need a real first and surname for this. Also check for different ways to spell a name for example Yucif or Usif. If you know his job, country of origin or location, type them in all together, if the name produces too many matches. For example:

Yucif Jazel – Tunisia

Or

Ucif Jazel – Tunisa

Or

Yucif Jazel – Manager at Sporty.com

Or

Ucif Jazel – Manager at Sporty.com

It takes some time but you must try variations and pay attend to detail.

2. Does he have a Facebook account?

This is a tricky one because I have come across a minimum of 3 different Facebook accounts in one go, for my ex fiancé but more about that later. The key here is that if you are lucky enough to locate an account and you see that his profile is zip up, which means you cannot share a picture, you cannot comment and you most definitely cannot see his news feed, that is one big red flag! What he is telling you and all the other women that he meets is, "you can't access me". Also be mindful that if all you see is sexy girl on his Facebook page, then be sure that is his 'catch a girl' page. This is quite common; these men think they are slick but it does not go that way once you know. The final killer punch is if he would not add you to his Facebook friends; that tells you he does not want to invite you into his world. Don't believe him when he says, "I'm not online often", pure lies - it's a dating app! The deceit from some of these men saddens me and then makes me angry enough to want to kiss and tell all. As long as I live, I will never forget Foster, he lived in my area and we dated for 3 months. He was a gentlemen and took the time to know me but would not add me to his Facebook. This went unspoken for a while, with me thinking, 'so it's alright to sleep with me and eat my food but you cannot allow me onto your Facebook?'. When I brought it up, he would just brush me off and laugh about it. In the end I called it off before my birthday because he was unwilling to commit to me and when it came down to it, I was just more of a convenience for him. He told me his deal-breakers were being overweight but wait, did Foster not meet me at this size? His other objection was that I used to smoke and I snored and he could not sleep but wait, Foster don't you snore? That experience knocked my confidence big time, I was depressed for 3 months solid because I made boundaries; sistergirl, I am just tired of this type of brother. There was a red flag right from the start though. When we first hit it off, we talked for 4 hours outside in my car on a hot summer's day and we clicked. He was travelling to a fitness bootcamp in Canada for two months and he promised to be in touch, when he returned in December. I waited and waited some more, Christmas came and went, New Year came and went. No contact, no calls. I knew he was back because he lived across the way and the lights were on. I later found out that he was holding out for some

Canadian woman but wait, there is more. Another red flag was when I visited him at home and prior to leaving, his behaviour was really inappropriate and that was when I really should have checked myself. Yet unfortunately for me, I was stuck in, 'he is fineeeeee and he is showing an interest'.

I guess at this point, I had to begin to look at why my confidence and self-esteem were so low when it came to the opposite sex. At some point I have to take responsibility for putting myself in ridiculous situations; it would be unfair to place all this blame on the man. So, this is when the reflection began and I started writing this book. I wanted to overstand implicitly what were my experiences saying about the way I see myself. What type of role models did I have around me and why was it okay for me to accept that I would feel paranoid, jealous or possessive in a man's presence, when he would trigger my childhood rejection and abandonment issues. This was really when I began to unpack and understand my addictive nature. Look, I could go on and one but let's move on Lady Detectives and I hope you are finding some value in what you read here.

3. Use google images and match his image

This is my favourite stake out of all, wow the wonders of technology. Google stores images of people online, with multiples photos. This means you can make a reference to whether you are being catfished, if an image comes up on your screen that looks very impressive. For example, Omari Hardwick, I knew he looked familiar but I had no idea he was an actor because I was confused when I was looking at a picture of Omari outside Brixton Tube Station in London, England. One day I'm watching television and I'm like, 'oh there is Trey' and then it all clicked into placed, I was being catfished by someone really mean who thought it was amusing to beguile women. I never knew about this technique then but I sure do now. Here is what you do.

<u>Type Google image in your search bar and wait for the camera image to appear.</u>

Then click on upload image, you will only be able to do one image at a time.

Google will either tell you there are no matches find, show a list of suggestions or locate the actual image. In this example, it is Omari Hardwick and you can follow through on any links. Unfortunately, I do not have the copyright to show you this man's handsome face but you can google him to satisfy your curiosity of what he looks like. Go on have a look, I know you will.

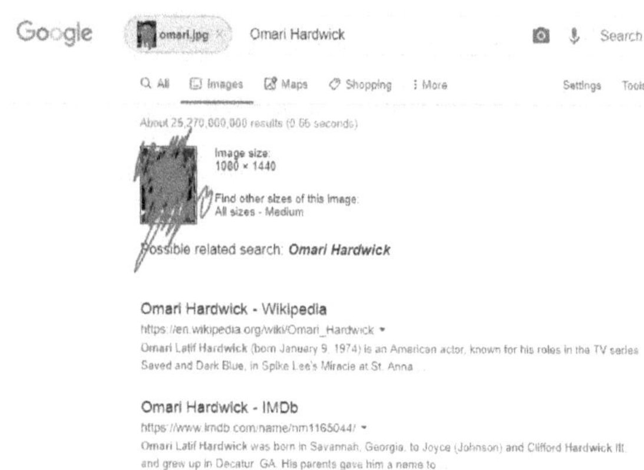

Google
omari.jpg
Omari Hardwick
Search
All
Images
Maps
Shopping
More
Settings
Tools
About 25,270,000,000 results (0.66 seconds)
Image size:
1080 × 1440
Find other sizes of this image:
All sizes - Medium
Possible related search: Omari Hardwick
Omari Hardwick - Wikipedia
https://en.wikipedia.org/wiki/Omari_Hardwick
Omari Latif Hardwick (born January 9, 1974) is an American actor, known for his roles in the TV series Saved and Dark Blue, in Spike Lee's Miracle at St. Anna ...
Omari Hardwick - IMDb
https://www.imdb.com/name/nm1165044/
Omari Latif Hardwick was born in Savannah, Georgia, to Joyce (Johnson) and Clifford Hardwick III, and grew up in Decatur, GA. His parents gave him a name to ...

4. Download Callapp onto your phone

This is the non-English version but for the purpose of demonstration, I will share. This app is so deep and I only found out about it in March 2019. Callapp identifies anyone on social media with a Google account. When unknown numbers call you or you are given a number from your prospect, simply tap it into the search engine and see what comes up. In my last check, I was able to see a Facebook page for Yusif and his Twiter handle. I could not find him by his fake name which was on the profile.

Rule #16: Double Facebook

Unfortunately for us, some men have more than one Facebook account. My former fiancé, Etcha, had three Facebook accounts. The first one had about 80 friends, which were mostly exotic looking females. He hardly posted on there. I did think it was a bit odd but later when questioned, he said that was his only account and became really defensive. The second <u>real</u> Facebook account with his family and friends, was discovered by accident. Due to the magic of the internet, one thing led to another and I saw a picture of him with his real name attached pop up in my feed. THINK ABOUT IT, straight up that is a red flag. I quizzed and grilled him over skype video and the cheeky sod said to me, "why do you want to be with someone you do not trust" and ended the call. I was mortified and there and then I should have walked away. Yet I stayed, telling myself that I must be paranoid and that I should learn to trust him more. He added me to his real page and we moved on from there. While on his Facebook page, I noticed he liked to change his name several times, this was before Facebook's new rules about genuine names came about. Again, in my online searches and looking through his messages, I found his third account - yes with a different name - and I thought to myself, 'this guy must just be a player'. This time he lied and said it was his friend's page, who had died. Throughout this time, I had a gut feeling something was not right.

I told you we were engaged to be married right? Well the outcome of that was he moved away to Brazil, contact became less and I ended it because I knew I deserved more. He unfriended me from Facebook and a couple of months later, I just happened to look on his page and was shocked to my core to see his girlfriend and six-month old son.

You see that inner voice inside, it is called intuition, pay attention to it ladies, it will be your guide. This is a true story. In the 18 months we were seeing each other, he got his best friend pregnant and she used to wave at me in the background of our video calls, on his laptop, pretending she didn't know English. A painful lesson to learn and my spliff intake simply increased.

Rule #17: How To Spot A Fake Profile

To the professional dater, aye this could be quite easy but newbies y'all better take some notes. Pay attention, here is the trick if you view a profile that has 3 to 4 top quality professional pictures making them look like a model. Chances are, they are *not* a celebrity. It is too unrealistic; just go and watch a few episodes of 'Catfish' on YouTube, if you do not believe me. A celebrity will have a massive online presence 'footprint'. Save their profile picture by screenshot and upload them into google image as I have taught you. You will see if they match and you can take your online search from there. When I was seeing Rick The Dick, I did this image search and found several pictures of him on another dating sites and I became instantly jealous. This included one picture of him in the shower, all soaped up. All the pictures show him off as happy and smiling but this is not the case. When you are a Sniper and paid to kill national threats for a living, there has to be a dark, killer instinct to you, somewhere you need to be cold and simply disconnected. He was a light sleeper and whenever I moved, he would wake up. Yet he manged to sleep through my snoring (directed at Foster), funny that. We will go through that episode of disasters later on in this book; just keep reading.

Rule #18: Nude Pictures

The minute you go on a man's profile and he has a topless picture of him or his buttocks with a partial towel over him, walk on by. Do you want hundreds of women eyeing up the intimate parts of your potential date? Demand more from your profiles, it will last longer if you separate the wheat from the tares. Plus, you should know by now that he is looking for a sexual hook up. Now if that is your thing, I'm not judging you sis, do your thang, different strokes for different folks. I am not mad at you.

Rule #19: Instagram links

Avoid attaching your Instagram page to your profile. I believe this gives men too much information on you and a huge insight into your personal life, they need to earn that level of trust. Of course, there may be men who are doing what I suggest here and doing their own detective work; fair play to them. I guess I cannot question my own advice! The exception to the 'no-instagram' rule, is if you can see a man's insta account, take a look, be inquisitive and again, become a detective. It tells you so much about his world. Look out for venue locations, areas he has visited or may have stayed, familiar locations and sights. Also remember some apps limit your viewing pictures to around 29 and you will need to go online for that. When it comes to the precious you thought, keep him guessing, do not be an open book, as my mother says, do not let the left hand know what the right hand is doing. I am not a fan of Insta connections on dating profiles, as it is too much too quick and I'm sure there are some dick pics in your DM's (direct messages) This wreaks desperation sis; it's a no from me.

Rule #20: Camera Angles

Elevated camera angles are a great way for hiding the ugly. If someone has the same type of picture, be suspicious. Also ask and see how recent the picture on their page is. Time changes so much and you do not want to meet a pot-bellied baldie, if he was sporting a six-pack back in the 90s; it is just not fair. Also, if you are voluptuous, elevated camera angles with a tilt, can be quite streamlining.

Rule #21: The Bed

Bed pics are a no-no; for obvious reasons, I'm a break this one down. Come on, think about it. A man with profile pictures of him laying down on the bed, with bedroom eyes, is a complete no. Computer says no. N-O spells NO and NO again!! What self-respecting man wants to show you his bed, does he have no shame? What would his mama say? Even if he is fully clothed, it's no from me, a HUGE turn off. What is he insinuating? It is really suggestive, maybe I am an old fuddy-duddy and you know what, I'm okay with that; a hot coco and my slippers thanks.

Rule #22: Torso Pick Of The Day

Now I am all for a six-pack, do not get me wrong. However, think about it, what woman wants her potential boo sharing his wares to the rest of the of the online community? Now, if you want to fuck then that is cool, go right ahead and do your thang. However, if you are looking for a serious relationship, no matter how buff that torso is, move on to the next. The exception is when he is working out in the gym and maybe you can see it through his clothes, that is less obvious.

Rule #23: Unmatch – Delete – Repeat

Look, let me break it down to you like this. If the conversation is boring you, or maybe he is taking too long to respond to your messages (yes, It might be the case that he seems to want to write a message forever). However, you are under no obligations to keep communicating. Simply unmatch him and move on. Life is a bitch and then you marry a bastard, the people we meet will never be perfect, so if you can secure 80% of what you want, you are off to a great start. Never be afraid to let a man go.

Rule #24: Unmatch – Report – Delete

If a guy starts speaking to you in an unappreciated manner during your text conversation, you have the power to block him. If he is being aggressive or sexually explicit, you do not need to entertain that behaviour.

Rule #25: The Rush Boo

Forget The Rush Boo, he is what we can also refer to as Mr Eager Beaver, we discuss him more fully later in the book. Ain't nobody got time for that. The quicker he falls in love with you, is the quicker he will fall out of love with you. If on day one, The Rush Boo is desperately trying to get your number, it is a sign to walk away.

Remember, the chances are he is doing this to every woman that he meets and your success rate of actually going on a date will be much lower because you did not build a rapport. Some men want to fill up their little black book, while others want to jump to a date quickly to see if they really like you but that is their insecurity, not yours. Then you have the ones that just want to pull your panties down real quick and give you the hot work! Put The Rush Boo to the test and see if he is really interested in getting to know you. When he asks for your number, reply with this message: *I am really flattered that you would want my number, however we only just started talking. Do you mind if we write for a little while longer?*

Two things will happen here. Number one, he will accommodate your wishes or number two, he will make it a big issue and it will dominate your text talks. You will need to either unmatch or delete his profile. Building relationships is like a fine wine, it takes time to mature. Slowly does it is the best, slow-burn option.

Rule #26: No credit, forget it

Look ladies, let's keep it real, ain't nothing going on but the rent. Call me superficial, I really don't care; if a grown ass, ashy foot, hardback man who's got a job has no credit to call you. Simply say to yourself, in the words of Beyonce, "to the left, to the left". Get out of there please, oh no, this will not do. I should not need to tell you this, do yourself a favour and step aside. Go to your address book, block, delete and repeat to any other no-credit-motherfucker. Hell, we are all going through hard times, I'm still going through hard times; what the heck do I look like calling him back, when we are all grown out here.

Rule #27: What A Suspect

If a man only calls you or messages you on WhatsApp it's a red flag. He is either too cheap to top up his phone, or he is desperately trying to save money. Look here, constant internet calls are well dodgy. How can you rely on him in a crisis, what is he going to say, "hold on let me see if I got internet to dial 999"? Get out of here. It is not uncommon for him to only give you a WhatsApp number only that does not dial, so what happens when he goes ghost? There is no recall action here. Be wary, sis.

Rule #28: Alcoholics Are Us

9 times out of 10 if a guy has a profile picture featuring an alcoholic drink, a bottle of wine or just plain old drinking from the bottle, chances are he could have alcoholic tendencies, issues or maybe be a full-blown alcoholic. What his profile pictures are telling you is that, "I am a good-time guy and I like to get pissed on every occasion I can." Getting

pissed and legless is his only objective in life and I hope you do not want to be a care-giver to someone who is co-dependant.

Rule #29: Light It Up

Spliff, spliff do you want a whiff, whiff? If a man has a joint hanging out of his mouth on his profile, he is telling from the start, "I take drugs." He is a straight up weed-head and unless that is what you are into, I suggest you exit, stage left. Ideally, you are looking for a mate who does not have any drug or alcohol dependency issue. You know I had a problem with weed right, well I used to be a chronic marijuana smoker - morning, noon and night. This is probably why my dating behaviour was super erratic most of the time. Maya Angelou says it perfectly, "when someone shows you who they are, believe them the first time".

Rule #30: Poor Hygiene

I find it quite repulsive to go on a date and a man has yellow plaque in his mouth. You expect me to kiss that, allow me. No fucking way. Yuk. Where the bucket? I'm going to hurl. All night on this date, I keep moving my tongue around my mouth like that was going to help him get rid of his plaque.

The worse thing is the stank smell of BO (body odour) it actually offends my nose. Do me a favour bruv, know where a bar of soap lives, you dutty boi! Are men not having showers anymore? It is absolutely rank.

Rule #31: Community Husband

Well blow me down with a feather, I am still shocked to this day that husbands do not take their wedding vows seriously. As God is my witness, today is 19th April 2017 (yes, it took me this long to publish this book) and through my Lady Detective skills, I discovered Mr Community Husband got married last year. It is splashed all over Facebook for the world to see; he was not hard to find at all. Why the heck would he be talking to me? Poor Mrs Community Husband, she in love thinking, 'I got me a good man, let the haters hate'. When to her ignorance, he is going around cheating on her with random lookalikes off the internet. I am disgusted, to be honest. The worst thing is, when I actually looked through his pictures, I remember images of him from his previous profile where he told me straight away that he was living with the mother of his children but they were not together. I thanked Mr Community Husband for being honest and told him I was not interested. We went our separate ways. I actually find men like this quite disturbing and what made it worse was when he moved to my area, he started going to my gym and I learned of this by looking at another gym member's profile and seeing them together. Again, can you see how easy it is to be deceived? You need to do your due diligence at all times. Protect yourself and protect your heart.

Rule #32: Non-committal

If a man says he is not ready for a serious relationship and just wants to have fun, listen to the words coming out of his mouth, as he means what he says. Do not trick yourself into thinking you can change him, we do not have enough pages in this book for the woman who thought she could change a man, so let's not even entertain that. When a man desires a woman, he will chase her.

Rule #33: One-Image Wonder

Never go on a date with a man with only one profile picture. He will be a Jekyll and Hyde, waiting to eat you alive. Verify who this stranger is.

Rule #34: Jelly Fishing

Some men, not all, can get jealous without meeting you. They start acting possessive from the gate, sending you mad messages like:

Are you there?

Why you taking so long to respond?

You are hardly ever online, give me your number.

I don't want you to talk to anyone else.

Are you talking to other guys?

Doh! It's a dating website, I am not going to talk to their nan am I? Of course I'm talking to other men, stupid. This is a tell sign that this man could be a protentional stalker.

Rule #35: Two Shades Of Purple Pain

When it hurts so bad and he is not calling you back; he is not responding to your texts in a timely fashion and is basically drifting away, let the bastard drift on. You will never have to beg any man that wants and desires you to stay and be with you. If you are torturing yourself in his absence, there is no need; get a life and finish reading the rest of this book. Build yourself back up, you are a survivor and you are worth more. Do you not know your royalty sis?

Rule #36: Me, Myself And I

One day I met a hot guy, who looked quite impressive on and offline, tick box. Yet there was one problem, yeah you guessed it. His ego was so massive that it eclipsed our entire conversations. I pointed out in the conversation that he knows nothing about me and he should learn to be more of an active listener. His response was he was super excited and I proceeded to talk about me. Guess what? He found a way to divert the conversation back onto him. It was a massive turn off. All is not lost because I convinced him that our relationship moving forward should be one that consists of business.

Rule #37: Ego Maniac

I met a guy who was....well, the best way to describe him is that he was peculiar. Mr Self Absorbed was a narcissistic piece of shit. He lived on his own planet and all he talked about was himself. It was so off-putting, he did not want to know anything about me. He kept interrupting me and when I talked about myself, he would turn the conversation back to him. Avoid men like him, even if you are a quiet lady, who is shy and retiring, do not be with someone who cares so little not to ask about you or your day. You are worth so much more, baby girl.

Rule #38: Taxi

I remember a so-called Surgeon (and yes that was to be debated) asking me, during a first date, what sexual positions I liked. I immediately took offense and went into one, he had pushed my buttons. I told him straight, it is inappropriate to speak to me in that way. His response was feeble and all, "come on, we are all adults here" and "how am I supposed to get to know you". Then he continued to reprimand me like a little girl, before driving me home. Telling me how I would always be single with that attitude. The safest option for me would be to hail a taxi at this point, as he was a creep.

Rule #39: Mr Eager Beaver

WATCH OUT!! Just like The Rush Boo, this predator is lurking and waiting for you to be his next prey, he is desperate and needy. Be very careful, you have been warned. **True stories:** three times in my adult life, I have met men who wanted to marry me to stay in the country. I call them Mr Eager Beaver. The most recent one was several years younger than me.

Day one: He tried to kiss me the first day that I met him.

Day two: He was in love with me.

Day three: He wanted us to have baby.

Day four: And on the fourth day, he wanted to get married.

I shit you not. He wanted me to meet his parents. Said we should get check out at the clinic for STI's and it was only after 3 weeks of dating. Ultimately, I was disappointed in myself, I believed that he loved me, yes silly, stupid girl that's me. I just want to be loved, I just needed a hug so bad that a man would say any bollocks and I'd just believe him. This was because there was a need in me that was not met in my childhood. I am still a work in progress but see this is why I was so frustrated and had to write this book. If I could at least save one woman from the grief and heartache that can derive from online dating, I would feel like I have achieved my purpose in life.

I said to Mr Eager Beaver, "love is not ignoring me and you stopped calling me for one whole week and no I don't want to have your child, we barely know each other." He followed this up with some lame-ass text saying, 'do you think we are gonna work out?' Fuck no, if you keep pressuring me like this, with your bullshit. Nowadays, Mr Eager Beaver is shacking up, playing house with another female and smoking weed; he never smoked when we first met, he was a gym fanatic.

I need some therapy right now because I swear, I need to heal the broken me. The wounded little girl inside me that was sexually abused by a man and a woman, needs to heal. Repairing the broken me is the best thing I can do for myself, it is loving, kind and nurtures me. Becoming emotionally fit means I can repel these eager statements from a man. At the bottom of it all, my need to love and to be loved has taken me so many dark places. That's why dating is a surprise because you never know what jack in the box crazy is going to pop at you next. When you see cray cray coming cross the street.

So, in short, avoid any man that wants to go at break neck speed to make you his woman or wife. A healthy relationship grounded in planet earth, will take it's time to blossom. My Pastor advised me to see a man through all four seasons before making long-term commitments like marriage.

Second

Base

Welcome to second base and congratulations that you have made it this far, it is a bloody miracle, considering all that we have been through. By now, you should be cooing over each other and arguing over who should hang up first. Whoa, slow down Nelly, there are still a few things that you need to know. Let's take a look at second base, now that it looks like things are sizzling between you two.

Rule #40: First Date

It is exciting times, you must be enchanted with each other by now. It is a must to meet in a public place, ladies. DO NOT accept any homecooked meals at his place. Make sure your date is two hours or less. Think about it, you want to keep him wanting more. Try cocktails, hot beverages or dinner at a push. Please do not get tipsy or drunk as you will lose your inhibitions and become complacent. Never overstay your welcome and always be the first to leave. Watch a few online body language videos and really learn if he is interested in you.

Rule #41: Kiss-Me-Not

It's a big "NO" from me. If you kiss a man on the first date, he is going to think you are a fast-ass woman. It gives the wrong impression of you, if you are looking for a serious long-term commitment. Politely decline, by turning your cheek and make your exit. Normally men will try and test you to see how far you go. Our job is to pass the test.

Rule #42: The Car

Do not get a man to pick you up from home when dating , you do not want him to know where you live yet until you have met his family, seen his home and he is showing a deeper level of getting to know you. Keep him guessing. Secondly, once you are in his car it could be potentially unsafe for the first few dates as you figure him out and it is an enclosed space for him to try and force himself on you and touch you up or lean in and kiss you. It is such a confined space. Be careful and not so accessible.

Rule #43: Disappearing Act

Do not alert the police when suddenly bae falls off the face of the planet. Ghosting from the opposite sex, is normal for up to 3 days. During this time, your bae is deciding if he wants to pursue things further with you and how much investment he is willing to make. Stay cool like a cucumber and wait it out. Anything after 3 days of no communication, he is taking the fucking piss and he has a few other chicks he is talking to. It not just you sis, these dating sites are notorious for this. It is probably safe to say he is losing interest. He has not lost your number and he is NOT laying half dead in a gutter somewhere and NO you do not call or text, by any means necessary. Fear not, this simply means he is not the one for you.

Rule #44: Video Calls

Once you have met in person and there is a strong connection or chemistry, you may open up to the world of video calling. This is quite a personal thing because you are inviting them into your space. Be warned of men sitting on the bed topless.

I had an awful experience with a man from Scotland who insisted we video chat. The dirty beggar was wanking off whilst I was video calling him. When I asked him what the fuck are you doing? His response was "it is normal thing to do". Hell no and especially not without my consent. The desperate prick, I wanted to smack him in is month. What a dick, excuse the pun, I was well pissed. He even offered to pay for my ticket to visit him.

It was quite distressing, unless of course, you are into that kind of thing. If so, then this book is not for you, go ahead and do what you want. I want to help women who have not done online dating before or women who need to know the ropes a bit better because they are currently not having much success.

Rule #45: Prospect Or Suspect?

Very quickly you need to learn how to discern a man's intentions towards you. You need to acknowledge whether he is a prospect or a suspect, by the way he responds to you. Once you can figure that out, you will be able to make informed decisions. Always consider this question: Is he a prospect or a suspect? Follow your instincts.

Rule #46: Fantasy Island

Liar, liar, pants on fire. Mr Pants on Fire had me hook, line and sinker. It was quite scary, anything he said, I believed him. We began dating and on our first date, he told me he was in a car accident. Silly me I believed him, of course this was the reason why he could not meet me for our first date. I could give you a list of lies from this man's mouth but we will be here all day, I'll save it for my next book of nightmare dating horror show. My mum always says time is longer than rope and sadly, I would later find out that he was a drunk and a gambler.

Basically, these men live in an elaborate fantasy that they believe to be real. Mr Pants on Fire promised to take me away on holiday, he said he was single but I found later out he had a wife, living in Luton actually. I walked from one lie into the other, I just could not understand why someone would lie. On another occasion, one of the many reasons why he could not meet me was his cousin died and he lost his mind and turned his phone off for a few days because he could not think straight. He admitted to me that he was a compulsive liar, so remember all that glitters is not gold. The last time I saw him was in East London, I was shopping and he was stumbling around drunk....and his breath was sour.

Rule #47: The Chase

MEN LOVE THE CHASE. You would be doing them a disservice if you did not allow them to pursue their role. Let the man chase you. Let him woo you. Let him pursue you. Let him sit and wonder 'why have I not heard from her'? Allow him to be the hunter, none of this new age 'independent woman' nonsense. In a relationship, men and women should be interdependent, however let's keep traditional courting alive.

Rule #48: RTNR (Ring Tone No Replay)

Sometimes ladies, you have to let the phone ring out. Do not always be so accessible to your prospect. You're not ignoring him, you are just letting him know you have a life.

Alternatively, if you find that you call him and he is not responding, leave him where he lays. You do not need to be chasing no man or calling him 3 or 4 times a day. I've been there, done it and that shit is just pushing them further away. Have some dignity and pride and accept that this may not work as you had first hoped. It is better to be a realist than to be disillusioned.

Rule #49: Blocked Caller

Remember you can use the block caller function if a guy is getting on your nerves. Do not feel obliged to speak with him if he is not your type, now that you have taken the time to know him better. You can block him on the phone and you can block him on the

WhatsApp. Take control of how you communicate.

Rule #50: The Midnight Caller

Unfortunately, I have done this before when I accepted calls late. My friend told me it does not look good. It sends over the wrong impression. It is the same for matching someone online and sending them a midnight message. My excuse was that I work shift hours, which was a lie but there is a time and place for everything. Make him call and communicate early evening. At midnight, his wife could be sleeping.

Rule #51: The Visa And Green Card Edition

Be mindful of men who promise you the world and want you to get married straight away. It is a scam, I tell you, do not fall for it.

Rule #52: The Power Of The P

Ladies let me be frank, pussy power is your best weapon in dating - period! No pun intended. Look here, the chase is all about men who want pussy juice, it is that simple. Technically, the longer you can keep them at bay, the better chance you have of seeing who is really serious. They want to climb on top of you and get in between your thighs and tell lies. Now that is real talk. Watch your back and watch your Vjayjay ladies. Make him work for the privilege to be by your side every morning.

Rule #53: Mental Health

Sis, be careful here please. I remember about 8 years ago, speaking with a guy from a website dating platform. He was pissing me off and I started giving him a bit of attitude and he told me that he used to beat up his ex-girlfriend for doing the same thing to him. I was silent, what more could I say? He went on to disclose that he had mental health problems in the past. That evening, he knew I was attending my friend's live open mic night in Brixton and it was an open event. He said he would join me. That was the quietest date I have ever been on; I am not about to get thumped in the mouth for snapping my neck and clicking my fingers.

Mental health is real within our community and we need to safeguard ourselves when out on our dates. Signs are not always visual. However, when Mr Wife Beater turned up, he just looked unkept and did not shave and he just kept glaring at me. It was really uncomfortable and I could not get out of it because I was singing that night.

I too have had my bouts with depression, where I sink into the pit of darkness; it was a very isolating time for me. One time, I did not wash for 3 days because my beloved DJ with his American accent, did not want to pursue a committed relationship with me. I stayed at home with my phone switched off, eating, drinking and smoking myself to death over an ex-con who had done jail time for attempted murder. Every so often, I would pass out and sleep; it was the only time I did not feel pain.

My dear friend, John had to come knocking on the door and tell me to get out of the funk I was in. Whilst he talked, I sat and I smoked weed, overate food and was drunk, watching

TV. I was a wreck over a man and I loved to isolate myself. Mental health can have some dark days, so you need make sure you are mindful of the different types of issues men may have, when meeting them for the first time. If you are not emotionally, mentally and spiritually strong, online dating is not for you.

Home Run

If you are lucky enough to reach this stage, you must be sure that you see a future together. You will find that you have more things in common than you do apart. This is a beautiful blissful time in a new relationship, when you decide to go steady. It makes you feel desired, loved and wanted. You get that warm fuzzy feeling inside, every time you see or think of bae.

By this time, you both should have closed down any multiple dating pages and agree to date exclusively. You will be in talks of us, we and togetherness, as you plan future activities. This stage is gooey and mushy; let's see if you can make it last for eternity.

Rule #54: Common Values

The late, great Whitney Houston sang, "We have something in common" and I know how relevant commonalities are, pertaining to growth in a healthy relationship. For example, active listening is a great tool you can have in a relationship but if it is not a value from both parties, this would need to be cultivated. If you both stand for integrity, effective communication and are supportive of each other's dreams, goals and aspirations, then this a great place to start. The following 12 core values should be incorporated when dating:

- **Assertive** -Show interest in your responses
- **Punctual** – Be on time and make a good first impression
- **Attentive** – Engage in the stream of conversation
- **Listen** – Pay attention, be an attentive listener
- **Passion** - Enthusiasm, Fun
- **Respect** - Self Love
- **Excellence** - Raise the bar higher
- **Responsibility** - Safeguard yourself on dates
- **Fairness** -Do not judge

- **Environment** – Be aware of your surroundings

- **Integrity** – Be open and honesty

- **Care** -Show genuine kindness

Rule #55: Family, Friends and Co-workers

You are onto a keeper if you are being introduced to his family, friends and co-workers. What this signifies is that he wants you in his world 100%, you are forever his girl, for now at least. There is not part of his life that he wants to keep a secret anymore. You have the keys to the kingdom, his heart and probably his wallet! The same applies to meeting his children in person; this example demonstrates that he is committed. You need not concern yourself with doubts that he will go astray because he is telling you by his open action that he wants you around.

Rule #56: My House Or Yours?

Knowing where bae lives is one the most insightful parts of building trust in a relationship. It shows a mutual understanding and at this stage you should be spending quality time together at each other's homes, texting daily and speaking sweet nothings over the phone. You would be lucky if the only challenge you face is when you say "you hang up, no you hang up first, no you. Okay on the count of 3". If that man trusts you enough to share his private bachelor pad with you, be sure to take full advantage of this. Being in his space will give you an insight into his world and what it would potentially be like if you were to live together. Ladies, I think we can exhale now.

Rule #57: Know Where He Works

It is so cute when on your holiday time off, you go and meet your man at his job for lunch. It is a great bonding opportunity and you may even get a chance to meet his work colleagues. This could be particularly insightful during a couple of minutes of simple conversations. I must reiterate that if he lets you into his world and you are able to find out more about him outside of the home environment, you are onto a winner.

Rule #58: Old Skool Landlines

When a man loves a woman, he doesn't mind being accessible and contactable at all times. It should be no sweat for him to give you his landline number (house phone). That way, if his battery is dead or phone is switched off in an emergency, you will be able to access him 24/7. This is great for building trust and feeling like someone has your back, at all times. Landline access rocks and yes, they are old fashioned but the point here is having accessibility, which is the key.

Rule #59: Touch Me, Tease Me

Do you remember back in the days of those slow jamz banging out the speakers, listening to TLC, Aaliyah, Justin Timberlake and Keith

Sweat? You knew it was time for your panties to come tumbling down your ankles. You might be chuckling now but you know I'm right. My best advice is to make sure that you feel comfortable at the rate of physical contact. Be mindful of one touch leading to sexual intercourse, you know the one when he says, "let me stick the tip in". Nine months later you will see where that tip leaves you. Make sure you articulate what is right for you. When a man really likes you, he will not pressure you for sex.

Rule #60: Heavy Petting

The more time you spend together, the closer you will get; kissing, touching, licking and sucking are all a part of that. You can have fun without penetrative sex. Make sure that you get a solid commitment from this guy before you go all out and give up the cookies, lady. Men like the chase, men like to feel like you are the catch of the ocean. He will wait patiently for you, if he thinks you are worth the energy and time.

Rule #61: The 3-Month Rule

Take it or leave it but relationship expert, Iyanla Vanzant says that being in a relationship is like test driving a car. You need to give it time to know if it is the right fit and 3 months together will help you understand each other's personalities, to consider if this is someone you want to take a road trip of life with. Plus, after 3 months the façade will fall, the mask drops and the real him should appear.

Rule #62: Choosing To Become Intimate

This is really a decision made by a couple who decide that they want to show their love via physical manifestation. Making love has the power to create a new life, be mindful that you are with someone who wants to go the long haul with you.

Rule #63: STIs Are Alive

Mumma always said, "it is better to be safe than sorry". Just take both your arses down to the sexual health clinic and get tested. Then you can have some freaky fun. Be certain that your partner is trustworthy sexually and has no other sexual partners. Remember your health is your wealth.

Rule #64: Four Seasons

Whoop tee do, you find your soul mate. Congratulations, it's a match. Before getting married consider this, wait 12 months before you say, "I Do". This gives you spring, summer, autumn and winter to decide if this person is right for putting a ring on your finger. This was great advice given onto me from my Pastor, when I was engaged in a long-distance relationship. By the fourth season, Etcha was gone; he cheated on me and had a son with a woman who to this day will not marry him.

Rule #65: Meet The Elders

When you are finally getting prepared to say your vows, it is always good to get chummy with the family first. Make sure you consult the elders in the family, so they feel part of the decision. This could be your Pastor, your rabbi or your grandparents. Their seal of approval is vital to your long-lasting relationship. Remember you are marring into his family, so you do not want any skeletons in his closet to come rattle you at night.

Dating Assessments

It is suggested that when you attend a first date, to make the following assessment which will help you evaluate what happened and will determine if it is right to go on your second date. It will allow you the time to figure out if this man ticks your vision board list of qualities. At the back of this book you will find some dating assessment templates to complete. Questions which require you to note your reflections of the date. There are other questions that may be answered with a sliding scale of 1 to 10 as below.

1____10

Poor **Good**

Good luck.

Dating Assessment Questions

On a scale of 1 to 10, how did your date go and why?

On a scale of 1 to 10, what was your compatibility like and why?

What is your level of attraction, on a scale of 1 to 10?

What 3 positive qualities could you find in your date?

Name 3 red flags you heard when he spoke? (think carefully about inconsistencies in his story)

What does your gut instinct tell you about your date?

What could you have done better?

What is his five-year plan?

Dating Assessment Questions

On a scale of 1 to 10, how did your date go and why?

On a scale of 1 to 10, what was your compatibility like and why?

What is your level of attraction, on a scale of 1 to 10?

What 3 positive qualities could you find in your date?

Name 3 red flags you heard when he spoke? (think carefully about inconsistencies in his story)

What does your gut instinct tell you about your date?

What could you have done better?

What is his five-year plan?

Dating Assessment Questions

On a scale of 1 to 10, how did your date go and why?

On a scale of 1 to 10, what was your compatibility like and why?

What is your level of attraction, on a scale of 1 to 10?

What 3 positive qualities could you find in your date?

Name 3 red flags you heard when he spoke? (think carefully about inconsistencies in his story)

What does your gut instinct tell you about your date?

What could you have done better?

What is his five-year plan?

Dating Assessment Questions

On a scale of 1 to 10, how did your date go and why?

On a scale of 1 to 10, what was your compatibility like and why?

What is your level of attraction, on a scale of 1 to 10?

What 3 positive qualities could you find in your date?

Name 3 red flags you heard when he spoke? (think carefully about inconsistencies in his story)

What does your gut instinct tell you about your date?

What could you have done better?

What is his five-year plan?

Dating Assessment Questions

On a scale of 1 to 10, how did your date go and why?

On a scale of 1 to 10, what was your compatibility like and why?

What is your level of attraction, on a scale of 1 to 10?

What 3 positive qualities could you find in your date?

Name 3 red flags you heard when he spoke? (think carefully about inconsistencies in his story)

What does your gut instinct tell you about your date?

What could you have done better?

What is his five-year plan?

Boy Meets Girl

Rick The Dick is such a long story; so much so, that I really need to write another book. I am going to keep it simple; this is the short and sour version, to give you an overview and insight into when a woman loves too much.

Boy meets girl.

Boy matches girl online.

Girl thinks boy is devilishly handsome.

Boy asks girl on a date.

Girl was running late.

Boy becomes very unhappy.

Boy is so upset, he cancels the date.

Boy keeps girl talking online for a year, to punish her date no-show.

Boy continues to Snapchat and video call girl.

Girl thinks boy is still interested in her.

Boy insists that girl comes to his home.

Girl declines.

Boy keeps in touch and repeats his home visit offers.

Boy and girl go back and forth.

Till finally..........

Girl goes to boy's house, to please boy.

Boy behaves himself.

Girl goes back again, again and again.

Girl becomes obsessed with boy.

Boy knows she is hooked.

Boy takes advantage of this information.

Boy is much stronger than girl.

To prove his strength, boy throws girl to floor to assume power.

Girl is defenceless.

Boy says he is playing.

Girl does not like this rough game.

Girl is unable to get up, until boy releases his firm grip.

Girl cannot see boy without an appointment.

Boy arranges a meet up with girl for New Year's celebration.

Girl gets ready to meet boy.

Boy cancels girl and goes out with friends instead.

Girl is upset and feels abandoned.

Girl stops calling boy.

Boy calls girl and apologizes and promises to do better.

Boy says he will take girl out for date night.

Girl reluctantly agrees.

Girl is coaxed into visiting boy again.

Boy uses one hand to squeeze girl's neck.

Girl can't breathe.

Girl is afraid for her life.

Boy says to girl, "I can dispose of your body and no one will know."

Girl realises she is not safe with boy.

Boy is not being nice to girl.

Boy lets go of girl's neck and shows how powerful he is.

Girl likes boy but…

Girl slowly begins to realise that boy does not like girl in the same way.

Yet girl still goes back.

Girl thinks she can change boy.

Girl is now infatuated.

Boy kisses girl and in the morning…

Boy pulls a gun out in front of girl's face.

Girl freezes.

Girl is frightened.

Boy laughs.

Boy says, "don't mess with me."

Girl cries on the inside.

Girl feels ashamed.

Girl has no confidence.

Girl has no one to talk to.

Girl is sad.

Girl wants to be loved.

Girl knows the boy is doing bad things to her.

Girl says she must be brave.

Girl finds the courage to walk away from boy.

The moral of the story is: love and value yourself always. It is better to be alone and happy, than to be with someone and miserable. Your self-worth must be a priority in the days, weeks, months and years to come.

RED FLAG:

WARNING SIGNS

To reiterate, here are the red flag warning signs that should make you raise an eyebrow or make you think, 'I smell a rat, something is rotten and I am going to trust my gut instincts.' If you see a red flag, girl you better take off your high heels and run as fast as you can to the hills. Never ignore red flags, as they only produce heartache further down the road of love.

Google Wally Britishh Red Flag video on YouTube upon which I draw inspiration for this chapter. It's quite funny, you may need your Jamaican friend to translate it for you.

Red Flag 1: I love you

When he says that on the first date, the first week or first month, get out of there chick. He is not sincere and does not respect the unification of love.

Red Flag 2: I want a baby

He is trying to trap you so that he can claim you, love you and leave you. When a man knows you desire children, any old lie can fall from his mouth. "We can get married and try for a baby", is what he said in order to get a passport and stay in the country. Shame on you; I declined. I want a baby, is not baby I want you!

Red Flag 3: Let's get married

Let's get married, this is not the romantic Jagged Edge song. It's natural for us females to want to order the fairy tale happy ever after that Disney promised us. There is nothing wrong with engagement and marriage goals. It's a simple desire of the heart. Right from the gate, if these are his lyrics, girlfriend he is running game on you. Real recognise real, you better pick up your shoes and run on now. You hear me?

Red Flag 4: Come round, I'll cook you dinner.

Bollocks. No way. No bloody way. Decline and tell him to piss off. Date and rape come to mind when I hear this nonsense. His cheap arse needs to take you out. Ladies it is not fuck Friday, train these men to treat you like the Queen you are, demand nothing less.

Red Flag 5: Avoid eager beaver men

Run rabbit, run rabbit, run, run, run. It's a trap, it's a setup, WATCH YOURSELF! Don't go there, don't believe the hype. It takes a man three months or more to develop deep feelings for you, which aren't necessarily equated to love. Maybe his mother deprived him of love, I don't know but it is not your job to address his traumas yet.

Look, I'm an old-hand at this and it saddens me to say, I've encountered all of these red flags. I tell you these things, so you don't have to suffer anymore. Save yourself another fucking heartbreak my girl. Don't believe the hype or be a foolish fool.

The Heart Repair Centre

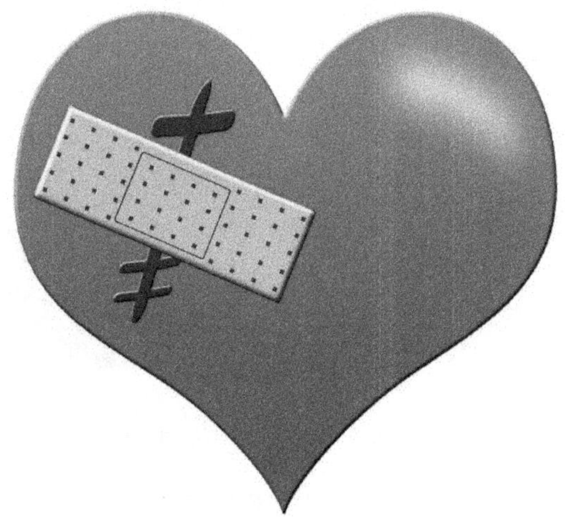

There comes a time in our lives, when we need to band-aid our bleeding hearts. We need to walk away when relationships don't work, won't work and when we most certainly need to heal. The heart repair centre is for the wounded dater, who just needs to take a breath.

It is time to look at what ails you. Ask yourself what patterns you are repeating? What story did you tell yourself as a child, about how you saw relationships? For me, poetry has always been a great way to express fractured feelings and matters of the heart.

Poem: Tasting Tears

(For Rick The Dick)

Sometimes I think of you when you're not
there

The way the moonlight shone upon your
soft, black hair

Your manly physique, keeping me warm at
night

A tingle in my spine, when you hold me tight

When you allowed me to look deep into your
face

The butterflies that tingle inside could never
be replaced

Then you grew darker and my feelings were
displaced

He *Loves* Me Not…

Treated me so cold, until it was my tears I could taste

The night that you choked me, made me so ill

To know that you are a killer and I could be killed

I thought maybe one day you could learn to love me

If you could get past the trauma of shooting dead bodies

You pointed your gun and aimed it straight at my heart

I felt so alive and then my world fell apart

Because your love is twisted, like acid in my face

He *Loves* Me Not...

You don't love yourself so it's a one-horse race

I accepted your lies even though they were bitter-sweet

I stand alone but at least I'm standing on my own two feet

I tried to excuse your behaviour away

Yet deep down I knew, you would kill me one day

If not with your smile, it would be with your rugged hands

You were the worst nightmare I've ever had

My dreams of us were built on sand

You left remnants of me feeling sad

Now I could tell stories of how we were all nice and polite

However, I'd be doing me a disservice and that ain't right

So ladies, trust me when I tell you I have been there

All because I wanted his attention, love and care

I found the courage to walk away

Non-existent self-esteem made me want to stay

To be honest, I struggle with this everyday

Wishing for the memory of us to go away

I still think of you every now and then

But our battle scares teach me to be my own best friend

Ladies take heed of my words, if he ever made you cry

Sometimes the sweetest lullaby is in
goodbye

The invisible hurt stays in the heart and mind

Wanting to be loved was my only crime

As he tussled me friskily to the floor

I knew the 'us' had faded and our
relationship would be no more

Buttercup

Ladies at the centre of you, is the gateway to your soul. It is the warm fragrant nectar of your fern garden and needs to be cultivated with love, by love, for love's sake. Know your worth and value on the inside first, for you are regal and wear a crown of virtue. Adorn yourselves with the beads of self-nurturing and strive for excellence daily. A balanced relationship is kind and must at all times, offer a retreat. Remember, you are a co-creator of life with God Almighty. That is why they call you wombman, a sacred woman enlisted to heal the massive! With arms open-wide, singing the ancestor's freedom song, you deserve abundance dear heart and may joy fill your days and peace calm your nights. Embrace your bountiful beauty, lady love.

Ladies Anthems

I created a song playlist on my 'He Loves Me Not' Ent YouTube account, to pick me up when I felt like shit after a dodgy date and was sick with continual emotional diarrhoea that goes nowhere.

No Scrubs - TLC

Heard It All Before – Sunshine Anderson

Survivor – Destiny's Child

I'm Good - Blaque

Caught Out There - Kelis

Rolling In The Deep - Adele

Breathe - Blu Cantrel

Get On The Bus – Destiny's Child

It's Not Right - Whitney Houston

Walk Away From Love – Bitty Mclean

Mama Knows...

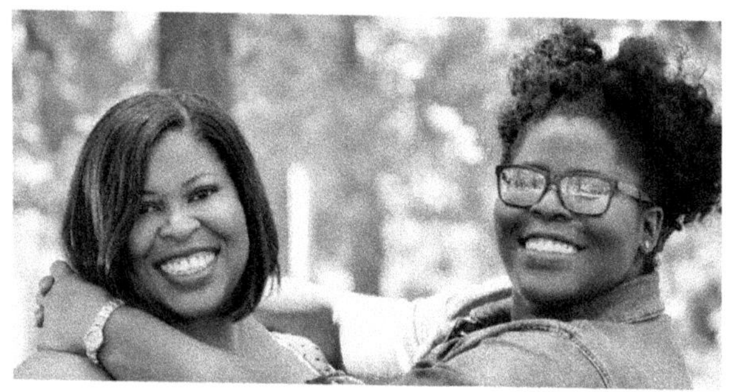

"Mama knows not to send the wedding invitations out, after the first date".

Mama knows pick sense out of nonsense.

Mama knows when he is a player, so listen to her words of wisdoms.

Mama knows the eyes are the window to his soul.

Mama knows when you should walk away.

Mama knows that all that glitters is not gold.

Mama knows that first impressions count.

Mama knows if he wants to go Dutch, he is watching his pennies and may not be a provider.

Mama knows patience is a virtue.

Mama knows do not show your hand.

Mama knows you should trust her because she can see up the street and around the corner.

Mama knows do not let the left hand know what the right hand is doing (yeah, I am still trying to figure that out).

Mama knows if he is back-peddling, proceed with caution.

Mama knows never chase what is running away from you.

Mama knows when he needs to take that bass out of his voice.

Mama knows when it is time to let go and let God.

Mama knows that one smart is dead at two smart door.

Mama knows that two smart is dead at three smart door (just figure it out).

Mama knows that a good man is not predicated on his good looks alone.

Mama knows that seasons change.

Mama knows the worth of the man is measured by the size of his heart.

Mama knows if it is not love, don't sweat it.

Epilogue

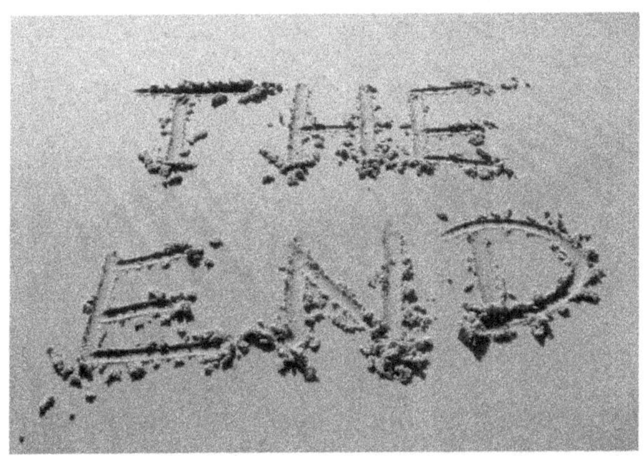

In love there are no guarantees, you need to be 100% authentically you in this process. Find someone who can unconditionally love you from the crown of your head, to the soles of your feet. Wait on your King lady, do not disappear. We are at the end of the He Loves Me Not book and at the beginning of a beautiful journey that can lead you to meeting your soulmate. It is time to bid you farewell on your dating adventure. My wish for you is that you find love within yourself, set your boundaries and believe that you deserve the best of what a relationship can offer. Avoid what I did; love *you* enough to demand respect, care and honesty. If this means some alone time, then so be it. The world will keep spinning, whilst you nurture yourself. You cannot pour water into a broken vessel, patch up the cracks that are in your heart. You are a winner, a precious gift from God. Believe that you are on the right track and the doors of opportunity must fly open. You can feel bad and recover. Tormenting yourself with twisted hearts is not your portion; you were born to manifest the best that life has to offer, in all areas of your relationships.

It has been fun to write this book, yet also cathartic and I have grown in the experience. I have had several conversations with my girlfriends, some married, some single and the general philosophy is this:

NEVER SETTLE FOR LESS THAN YOU DESERVE!

About The Author

Meet Winsome Duncan, who is a Book Confidence Coach and an award-winning entrepreneur. As the Founder of Peaches Publications, her book publishing experience spans more than a decade and she is passionate about books. Winsome is a bestselling author with ten books in her repertoire. Winsome's written television work has featured on BBC iPlayer, SKY, Virgin TV and BBC London radio. As a motivational speaker, Winsome was trained by motivational speaker, Les Brown and has trained with the UK's top speaker, Andy Harrington.

As an artist, she goes by the name 'Lyrical Healer' and is currently promoting her new single 'Marley', which is a tribute track to reggae icon Bob Marley, taken from her EP 'Get Up 3000'.

Her books are highly acclaimed, having received national press and media coverage and Winsome has been endorsed by former Minister of Justice, Sir Simon Hughes. Winsome resides in London, England and says writing is her passion and purpose in life. She continues to aspire to get the community writing and telling their stories.

Winsome's book publishing specialisms are:

- Editing
- Proofreading
- Ghost Writing
- Book Cover Design
- Copyright Protection
- Kindle Digital Upload
- Book Confidence Consulting

- Amazon Distribution Channels
- Paperback and Hardback Books
- Critical Friend Manuscript Analysis
- Book Structure Assessment and Analysis

Send us an email and let us know what you thought about He Loves Me Not. Do sign up for Peaches Publications newsletters, here also:

www.peachespublications.co.uk.

Getting Support

If you are affected by any of the issues in He Loves Me Not..., know that you are not alone. Please check out some of the support services that could be of assistance:

www.mind.org.uk

www.talktofrank.com

www.samaritans.org/how-we-can-help-you/contact-us

www.aa.org (Alcohol)

www.ca.org (Cocaine)

www.marijuana-anonymous.org

www.na.org (Narcotics)

www.coda-uk.org (co-dependent behaviour)

Notes

Notes

Notes

Notes

Notes

Notes

Notes

Notes

Notes

Notes

You Were Supposed To
LOVE ME
The Break Up Book
WINSOME DUNCAN
Photograph by RMClarke Photography

SO, YOU THINK I'M SUPERWOMAN?
TO THE LEFT, TO THE LEFT
Nicole Reid

www.ingramcontent.com/pod-product-compliance
Lightning Source LLC
Chambersburg PA
CBHW070954040426
42443CB00007B/508

* 9 7 8 0 9 5 5 4 8 9 0 8 2 *